WINNING WITH GOD

David S. Philemon

Royal Diadem Publishing Inc.

Dedication

To the Almighty God, my Rock, Refuge, and Source of all wisdom and strength. Thank You for Your unwavering love, grace, and the purpose You've placed within me. May this book bring glory to Your name and draw others closer to You.

And to my beloved spiritual parents, Dr. Paul and Dr. Mrs. Becky Paul Enenche, who have faithfully nurtured and guided me in this journey. Your example of unwavering devotion, godly counsel, and compassionate care has been a beacon of light and strength in my life. Thank you for standing as pillars of faith and for your steadfast commitment to the Kingdom.

ACKNOWLEDGMENTS

This book would not have been possible without the unwavering support, dedication, and talent of an extraordinary team. My deepest gratitude goes to each of you for your contributions, insights, and encouragement throughout this journey.

First and foremost, thank you to Rev. Mimi Philemon my dear wife, Rev. Shina Gentry, and and my assistant pastor Rev. Bright Amudoaghan for your incredible effort, encouragement, and belief in this project. Your support has been instrumental in bringing this vision to life.

To the dedicated leaders of Royal Diadem Publishing, Ide Imogie and Kishawna Bailey, I am immensely grateful for your belief in this project from the very beginning and for investing your time and energy into its development. Your creativity, dedication, and expertise have been the backbone of this endeavor.

I am especially grateful to the Royal Diadem Publishing team— Beulah Orogun, Emmanuella Ben-Eboh, Doyinsade Awodele, Kim Matthews, and Shante Gill, for your meticulous attention to detail, refining every page and ensuring that each word reflects our vision.

A heartfelt thank you to my family, friends, and colleagues whose unwavering support and belief in this project gave me the courage and strength to see it through.

Finally, thank you to all the readers and supporters who make this work meaningful. I am humbled and honored to share this journey with each of you.

With all my gratitude,
David Philemon

CONTENTS

INTRODUCTION

Understanding The Journey With God

L ife is like a journey, full of ups and downs, victories and challenges. But our journey has a whole new meaning when we walk with God. We aren't just moving through life by ourselves. We have a powerful partner—God Himself—who leads, guides, and shows us how to win, no matter what comes our way.

This book, "*Winning with God*," is about discovering how we can walk through life with God by our side and experience real victory. Winning with God doesn't just mean being successful in how the world thinks of success. It's much more profound. It's about living a life that pleases God, impacts others, and fulfills His unique purpose for us.

God has a plan for each of our lives. He created us with a purpose and wants us to live in a way that brings out our best. Jeremiah 29:11 tells us that God has *"plans to prosper you and not to harm you, plans to give you hope and a future."* But it's up to us to trust Him and follow His lead.

This book will show how to position yourself to receive everything God has promised. Sometimes, we might feel like we've hit a roadblock or don't know how to take the next step.

That's where this journey begins. When you learn to walk closely with God, the things that once seemed impossible will start to make sense, and you'll find new strength and direction.

Walking with God requires that we listen to Him and follow His instructions. Sometimes, God has secrets—things He's working on or preparing for us. But He doesn't always reveal these secrets to everyone. God shares His heart and plans with those ready to handle them.

This book will teach you what it means to mature in your faith so that you can hear God's voice clearly and be trusted with the unique things He wants to show you. Abraham, one of the great men of faith in the Bible, had this relationship with God. In Genesis 18:16-19, we see that even though God was on His way to do something meaningful, Abraham moved to stay connected with Him. Abraham's relationship with God was so strong that God decided to share His plans. This teaches us that God doesn't just want to give us blessings; He also wants us to be part of His plan to bless others.

When discussing winning with God, we're not just talking about material success or fame. We're talking about living a life that honors God, fulfills our purpose, and helps others. True victory means overcoming obstacles with God's help, growing in our faith, and becoming someone who impacts the world for good.

"*Winning with God*" means learning to hear His voice and follow His guidance. Being consistent in your walk with Him, even when things get tough. He was growing in spiritual maturity, living out the principles of your faith every day and generously sharing the gifts, talents, and blessings God has given you with others. This book will examine these themes in detail, providing practical steps and real-life examples to inspire you. You'll discover that there's no such thing as defeat with God. Even when things don't go as planned, God has a way of turning every situation around for good.

In today's world, getting distracted or overwhelmed by life's challenges is easy. But "Winning with God" reminds you that God has a better plan for your life. He wants you to win in some areas and every part of your life. Whether it's in your personal growth, your relationships, or your purpose, God is ready to help you overcome obstacles and find true success.

As you read this book, I encourage you to open your heart to what God wants to show you. This is not just a book of ideas; it's a guide for living a victorious life with God at the center. I pray that you will be encouraged, strengthened, and equipped to live in a way that pleases God and brings out the best in you. Let's take this journey together and learn what it means to win with God!

CHAPTER ONE

THE CALL OF ABRAHAM

"Then the men rose from there and looked toward Sodom, and Abraham went with them to send them on the way. And the LORD said, 'Shall I hide from Abraham what I am doing, since Abraham shall surely become a great and mighty nation, and all the nations of the earth shall be blessed in him? For I have known him, so that he may command his children and his household after him, that they keep the way of the LORD, to do righteousness and justice, that the LORD may bring to Abraham what He has spoken to him." Genesis 18:16-19

God's Initiative in Our Lives

God is actively involved and working to guide us. He does not leave us to figure everything out on our own. From the beginning, God has reached out to humanity, seeking a relationship with us. This is evident in the creation story, where He walked with Adam and Eve in the Garden of Eden (Genesis 3:8). God desires to connect with each of us personally and intimately. One of the clearest examples of God's initiative is in Abraham's life.

In Genesis 12:1-3, God calls Abraham out of his homeland, promising to make him a great nation and to bless all families of the earth through him. This call was entirely God's idea. Abraham did not earn or ask for it; it was a divine invitation. This story teaches us that God has specific plans for us and often takes the first step in revealing those plans. In our relationship with God, it is essential to remember that He seeks us out. Jesus emphasizes this in John 15:16, where He says, "*You did not choose Me, but I chose you.*" This means that God loves us first and desires a relationship with us. He is not waiting for us to come to Him but actively inviting us into His presence. This can be seen in various ways, such as through prayer, worship, and the prompting of the Holy Spirit in our hearts.

When God reaches out to us, He brings promises. God has good plans for our lives. He initiates these plans out of love and a desire for us to flourish. No matter where we are, we can be assured that God is thinking of us and has a purpose for our future. When we acknowledge God in our decisions, He provides direction and clarity. He may guide us through Scripture, prayer, or the counsel of others. This guidance expresses His love, showing He wants what is best for us. While God takes the initiative, our response is crucial. When God calls us, we must choose to respond with faith. This means stepping out of our comfort zones and trusting that He knows what is best. In Isaiah 6:8, we see a powerful example of this response: "*Also I heard the voice of the Lord, saying: 'Whom shall I send, and who will go for Us?' Then I said, 'Here I am! Send me.*" We actively participate in His plan when we say yes to God's call. Understanding God's initiative in our lives changes how we view ourselves and our purpose. It frees us from the pressure of earning God's love or approval. Instead, we can rest in the knowledge that Him chose and valued us. We are called to live in response to His initiative, trusting that He has equipped us for the journey ahead.

Just as God chose Abraham to be the father of many nations, He chose each of us for specific purposes. This choice is not based on how good we are, our talents, or how much we believe. Instead, it comes from God's perfect will and plan for our lives. God chose Abraham because He had a particular purpose for him. In Genesis 12:1-3, God calls Abraham and tells him to leave his homeland

and go to a new place. God promises Abraham that he will become a great nation, and through him, all families of the earth will be blessed. This shows us that God had a plan for Abraham even before he knew it.

Abraham's choice to follow God's call was a step of faith. He didn't know where he was going, but he trusted God. This teaches us an important lesson: God often asks us to take steps of faith, even when we cannot see the whole picture. When we respond to God, we become part of His bigger story. Like Abraham, each of us has a unique purpose in God's plan. Ephesians 2:10, *"For we are His workmanship, created in Christ Jesus for good works, which God prepared beforehand that we should walk in them."* God has made us with a purpose in mind. He has prepared good things for us to do.

Our job is to discover and fulfill those purposes. God's choices are intentional and loving. He knows what is best for us and wants to use us in ways we might not understand. This means we don't have to worry about our abilities or shortcomings. God equips us for the tasks He calls us to. God doesn't just sit back and wait for us to find Him. He actively seeks us out. He initiates relationships with us because of His love. God's love is the foundation of His choice. He wants us to know Him and experience His goodness. He invites us into a relationship where we can grow, learn, and become who He created us to be.

While God initiates the relationship, He also invites us to respond. This means we need to actively participate in what He is doing. As Abraham responded with faith, we are called to step out in trust. Our response matters. In James 1:22, we are encouraged to *"be doers of the word, and not hearers only."* This means we must act when we hear God's call or receive His promises. It's not enough to believe; we must live out that belief daily. Our response determines how much we experience God's promises. When we trust Him and follow His guidance, we open the door to His blessings and plans. This doesn't mean life will be easy, but it means we will walk with God through every situation. We often want immediate answers and quick solutions.

However, God's timing is perfect. Isaiah 55:8-9, *"For My thoughts are not your thoughts, nor are your ways My ways."* God sees the bigger picture that we cannot always understand. He knows what is best for us and when we are ready. Just like Abraham had to wait many years to fulfill God's promise, we may also need to wait. During this waiting period, God often works in us, preparing us for what will come. He teaches us patience and reliance on Him and strengthens our faith.

Abraham's story reveals the nature of God's relationship with His people. God desires a relationship that is deep, personal, and built on trust. He did not just command Abraham and leave him to figure things out. Instead, God continually guided Abraham, revealing secrets, making promises, and testing his faith. This close relationship allowed Abraham to partner with God in ways that impacted the world. God desires a similar relationship in our lives—one where He can share His plans, reveal His purpose, and involve us in His work. However, as in Abraham's case, this relationship requires maturity, faith, and obedience.

The Role of Prophecy in Our Journey

"You have to make sure your prophecy with God is intact. God will make you His mouthpiece or solution on the earth to play a major role in their redemption."

Prophecy is a powerful tool God uses to communicate His plans and intentions to us. In essence, prophecy is about predicting future events and God revealing His divine purpose and direction for our lives. Just as God spoke to Abraham, promising he would become the father of many nations, He also shared His plans to guide us along our journey. This prophetic insight helps us align our actions with His will and reminds us of His destiny in store for us.

For Abraham, the prophecy he received from God was life-changing. It wasn't just an abstract idea but a specific calling defining his existence. This promise shaped his decisions and actions, encouraging him to step out in faith even when the circumstances seemed impossible. Abraham had to leave his homeland, trusting in God's word, demonstrating that prophecy can lead to significant life changes. His promise to be a father to many nations motivated him to follow God's calling despite his challenges.

In our own lives, prophecy functions similarly. It can guide us, showing us the path we should take. When we receive a prophetic word, it often comes with the assurance that God has a plan for our future. This assurance can provide comfort and encouragement, especially in times of uncertainty. Just like a roadmap helps us navigate unfamiliar territory, prophecy helps us make decisions aligned with God's will. It gives us a glimpse into the future, reminding us of what we can achieve when we trust Him. It's important to understand that when God speaks a prophetic word over our lives, it is not just a prediction of what will happen. Instead, it is a divine invitation for us to participate in fulfilling His plans.

God desires us to be active participants in unfolding His promises. This means that prophecy is not passive; it calls us to engage in faith, prayer, and action. We must respond to the prophetic word by trusting God, praying for His guidance, and taking steps that align with His will. Knowing a prophetic word is not enough; we must act on it. This involves trusting God even when we do not see immediate results or taking practical steps toward fulfilling that word. For instance, if you receive a prophecy about a future calling, you may need to pursue education, seek mentorship, or develop specific skills. This proactive approach shows that we believe in God's promises and are willing to do our part to see them fulfilled.

Keeping Your Prophecy Intact
When God made a promise to Abraham, it wasn't just an empty statement but a declaration of His plan for Abraham's life.

However, for that prophecy to come to fruition, Abraham had to take steps of faith. This teaches us that our response to God's promises is crucial in their fulfillment. As gardeners tend to seeds to ensure they grow, we must actively nurture the prophecies spoken over our lives. This involves keeping our hearts and minds open to God's leading. We must regularly revisit the prophetic words we've received, allowing them to inspire and guide us. This is not a passive waiting game; instead, it requires intentionality. We should meditate on these promises, pray over them, and remind ourselves of them, especially during challenging times when doubts may arise.

God does not give us prophetic words just for them to sit idle. He imparts them to encourage and motivate us. Prophecies are meant to act as a beacon, helping us stay focused on His plans for our lives. They are reminders that God is at work, even when we cannot see it. Holding onto God's words is vital when we face difficulties or obstacles. These promises are a source of strength, reminding us that He has a purpose and a plan for us. Abraham's story illustrates that while God gives prophecies, there is still a role for us to play.

Abraham didn't just sit back and wait for God's promises to pass. He made intentional moves to align himself with God's will. When we receive a prophetic word, we must ask ourselves, "What can I do to bring this prophecy to life?" This could mean taking practical steps, such as pursuing education, praying, or making lifestyle changes that align with God's plans. Abraham's journey with God was marked by a desire to be in a close relationship with Him. Abraham became more attuned to God's voice and guidance as he walked with God. This relationship deepened his understanding of the prophecy he received. Similarly, we must cultivate our relationship with God, allowing Him to guide us as we walk in faith. The closer we draw to Him, the more precise our understanding of His plans will become.

As Abraham took steps of faith, God responded by revealing

His plans to him more. This shows us that God often provides further insights and revelations as we act on the prophecies we've received. When we take steps in faith, God may unfold new layers of His promises, leading us to a deeper understanding of His purpose. Therefore, staying proactive and engaged in our spiritual journey is vital. It can be easy to lose sight of our prophecies, especially when life gets complicated or we encounter setbacks. However, maintaining focus on God's plans requires discipline and perseverance. We must constantly remind ourselves of the promises He has made. One way to do this is through journaling, where we can write down the prophecies we receive, the insights God gives us, and the steps we take in response. This practice can help us see God's faithfulness over time.

Maturity and Prophecy
God may keep certain truths hidden from us because of our spiritual immaturity. In Hebrews 6:1-12, the Bible highlights that while salvation brings us into a relationship with God, it also introduces us to a growth journey. Some deeper truths and blessings accompany this salvation, but they are reserved for those who have matured in their faith. Spiritual maturity is not simply about how long we have been believers; it is about how deeply we trust God and our willingness to follow His guidance. For Abraham, maturity involved trusting God's timing, even when circumstances seemed impossible. It required him to be patient, faithful, and obedient, even when he faced challenges.

Abraham's journey teaches us that maturity is about developing a solid relationship with God, where we learn to rely on Him entirely. Just as a child grows and learns to trust their parent, we must grow in our faith and understanding of God. This growth is essential to receive and fulfill the prophecies spoken over our lives. Before we can be entrusted with more extraordinary revelations and prophetic words, we need to master the foundational principles of our faith. These elementary teachings include understanding God's love, grace, and forgiveness and how to pray, read the Bible, and serve others.

Like in school, where we must grasp basic math before tackling advanced calculus, we must solidify our understanding of these foundational truths in our spiritual journey. As we grow in these areas, we become more capable of handling the weight of God's promises. Maturity also means recognizing that God's timing is often different from ours. Abraham had to wait many years before the promise of becoming a father was fulfilled. This waiting period was not a punishment but a time for Abraham to grow in faith and understanding. During these waiting times, we can be tempted to doubt or take matters into our own hands, just like Abraham did when he tried to fulfill God's promise through his servant Hagar. However, true maturity lies in trusting God even when we don't see immediate results. Another aspect of maturity is learning to be patient and faithful in our daily lives. This means living out our faith in our actions, even when we are not yet seeing the fruits of God's promises. For Abraham, this involved daily choices to follow God, worship Him, and live righteously.

In our lives, we are called to demonstrate our faith through our actions, showing that we believe in God's promises even when the circumstances do not reflect them. Obedience is a critical indicator of spiritual maturity. Abraham's obedience to God was evident throughout his journey. He followed God's directions, even when challenging or requiring great sacrifice. Similarly, our willingness to obey God's commands reflects our level of maturity. God tests our obedience not to see us fail but to help us grow. Each act of obedience prepares us for the next step in our journey and makes us more receptive to God's prophecies and plans for our lives.

CHAPTER TWO

THE SECRETS OF GOD

"God has so many secrets, so much HE is doing and wants to say, but HE is keeping it back from so many. Why does God keep back secrets from so many? God tests you to see how you handle secrets, and then he tests you to see what you will do with other secrets."

The Hidden Things of God

God holds certain things in mystery, hidden from the majority but revealed to those who walk closely with Him. *"There are things God says to people that he hides from others."* Deuteronomy 29:29, *"The secret things belong to the LORD our God, but the things revealed belong to us and our children forever, that we may follow all the words of this law."* God has secrets. Still, He also reveals certain things to us as we grow in our relationship with Him. The hidden things of God are not meant to frustrate us but to deepen our faith and reliance on Him.

God has mysteries that He chooses to keep secret for His reasons, and these secrets can serve as an invitation for us to draw closer to Him. They encourage us to seek Him more earnestly, trusting His wisdom and timing. While we may wish to know all the answers, it's important to remember that God, in His sovereignty, understands that not everything needs to be revealed to us. Some aspects of our spiritual journey may remain a mystery because God knows that understanding them could overwhelm or distract us from what is truly important.

In times of uncertainty, we are encouraged to rely on God's character and faithfulness. Rather than seeing these hidden things as obstacles, we can view them as opportunities for growth. They prompt us to ask questions, seek answers through prayer and Scripture, and cultivate a deeper relationship with God. God's secrets are closely connected to His will for our lives and greater plans for humanity. They encompass both the specific directions He has for us and the broader mysteries of His kingdom. For example, we might not know why particular challenges arise, but we can trust that God uses those challenges for our growth and His purpose. The more we lean into God's Word, prayer, and obedience, the more He reveals His plans and purposes to us.

Reading and studying the Bible allows us to uncover truths about God's nature, promises, and desires for our lives. We become more attuned to His voice and guidance when intentionally seeking Him. God desires a relationship with us; through this relationship, He can unveil more of His secrets over time. Sometimes, we wonder why God doesn't reveal everything to us simultaneously. Wouldn't it be easier if we knew exactly what would happen?

However, God, in His infinite wisdom, keeps certain things hidden for our benefit. Part of this is because we are not always ready for the whole picture. God is doing things behind the scenes that we may not understand, but they are for our good. Just as a parent gradually reveals more responsibilities to a child as they grow, God reveals His plans to us as we mature spiritually. The hidden things of God require trust on our part, knowing that He is always working for our good, even when we don't fully see or understand His hand at work.

Why God Keeps Secrets
One of the most critical aspects of understanding God's secrets is recognizing why He keeps certain things hidden. It's not that

God withholds good things from us but that He knows when we are ready to handle deeper truths. One of the reasons God keeps certain things hidden is to test our readiness. He observes how we handle the knowledge and truths we've already received before revealing more.

In Luke 16:10, *"he who is faithful in what is least is faithful also in much."* This principle not only applies to material possessions but also to spiritual insights and revelations. God wants to ensure that we are mature and responsible enough to handle the more profound things of His kingdom. God often starts by giving us small tasks or limited understanding. How we manage these more minor responsibilities shows our readiness for more incredible things. If we faithfully apply what we already know, live in obedience, and demonstrate faith, God will trust us with more. He looks at how we live out our faith daily—whether we are sincere, consistent, and dedicated to His commands. When we show that we value what He has revealed, He may open the door to even greater spiritual truths. Before God unfolded the full extent of His promise to make Abraham the father of many nations, He tested Abraham's faith and obedience.

One of the most significant tests came when God asked Abraham to leave his homeland without knowing exactly where he was going (Genesis 12:1-4). His willingness to trust God showed Abraham's readiness, even when the complete picture was unclear. Later, when God asked Abraham to sacrifice his son Isaac, Abraham's faith was once again tested (Genesis 22:1-12). These testing moments showed God that Abraham was prepared to handle the more extraordinary promises and revelations that lay ahead.

In our spiritual journey, God often follows a similar pattern. He reveals enough to guide us but keeps certain things hidden to see how we respond to what we already know. We can receive more of His secrets if we show spiritual maturity by being obedient, patient, and faithful. However, neglecting the truth we've already been given shows we may not be ready for more.

Testing our readiness also helps us grow spiritually. When we face tests of faith—such as waiting on God's timing or obeying Him in challenging circumstances—we develop patience, perseverance, and a deeper trust in His plan. These qualities are essential for handling the greater responsibilities and revelations God has for us. Every time we pass a test, we move closer to fulfilling God's purpose for our lives and understanding His more profound mysteries.

God's tests are never meant to harm us but to strengthen our faith and prepare us for more. He uses these moments to refine our character and ensure we align with His will. God entrusts us with more significant assignments, wisdom, and profound revelations as we prove our faithfulness in small things. These tests are not just about what we can handle but about shaping us into the people God wants us to be. Another reason God keeps secrets is tied to our maturity.

Spiritual growth is a process, and just as children aren't ready for adult responsibilities, we are not always prepared for the weight of certain divine revelations. Hebrews 5:14, *"But solid food is for the mature, who by constant use have trained themselves to distinguish good from evil."* God reveals more to those who have developed spiritually, those who have mastered the foundational elements of faith and are ready for the "solid food" of more profound truths. It's not that God withholds good things but that He is waiting for us to grow into them.

In Hebrews 6:1-2, we are called to move beyond the elementary teachings about Christ and be taken forward to maturity. This means that while the basics of faith—like repentance, baptism, and laying hands—are essential, they are just the beginning. We must grow beyond these foundational truths and become spiritually mature to win with God.

Maturity in the Christian life is not just about knowing more facts about God; it's about applying those truths in everyday life. It's about living so that our actions, thoughts, and words reflect Christ. It's about consistently making decisions that align with God's will, even when difficult. For example, maturity means that when faced with trials, we trust God's sovereignty instead of panicking. It means we can disciple others, helping them grow in their faith. A sign of spiritual maturity is that our lives are a testimony to others—our faith becomes contagious, and others are drawn to God through our example. *"Maturity is turning your salvation into discipleship. How do you know you have mastered certain spiritual things? If your life is constantly disciplining another life."*

Salvation begins our walk with God, but discipleship is growing deeper in our relationship with Him and becoming more like Christ. It's not enough to be saved; we are called to become disciples, fully committed to following Jesus in every area of our lives. Discipleship means that we are learners—always seeking to grow, always open to correction, and always willing to be used by God to teach others. When we move from being saved to actively disciplining others, we begin to step into greater spiritual maturity. We are no longer just receiving; we are giving, pouring into others, and helping them grow in their journey with God.

So, how do you know you've reached a certain level of spiritual maturity? One clear sign is that your life is consistently disciplining others. When you can take what God has taught you and pass it on to someone else, you are walking in maturity. Additionally, maturity is seen in how we handle the challenges and secrets God gives us. God will entrust us with more if we can be trusted with small revelations and responsibilities. Spiritual growth is not a destination but a continual journey. As we mature, God will reveal more of His secrets to us, trusting us to handle them with care and use them for His glory.

Trustworthiness in God's Eyes
Before God entrusts you with more—responsibilities, revelations,

or spiritual insights—He often tests your faithfulness in what you have already been given. These tests assess your readiness for more excellent assignments and blessings, much like how a teacher provides tests to measure a student's progress. Trust is not just given; it is earned through obedience, consistency, and stewardship. Luke 16:10 emphasizes the importance of being faithful in small tasks: *"Whoever can be trusted with very little can also be trusted with much."* This principle reveals how God operates in His kingdom.

Our small responsibilities or opportunities provide a proving ground for more considerable blessings. If we handle these with integrity, diligence, and care, God knows He can trust us with more significant roles or revelations. For example, if God has called you to serve in a humble role—perhaps leading a small group or helping someone in need—how you respond in these moments demonstrates your readiness for more excellent leadership. It's not the task size but the heart and faithfulness with which we approach it that God values.

God often tests how we handle the truths and revelations He gives us. Proverbs 25:2, *"It is the glory of God to conceal a matter; to search out a matter is the glory of kings."* God entrusts us with certain revelations or insights, but how we manage these reveals our character. Are you quick to share things prematurely? Are you using divine insights for personal gain or recognition or guarding them with wisdom and discernment?

Handling revelation with care means waiting on God's timing, understanding His purpose for sharing it with you, and applying it for His glory—not your own. Just as Jesus often revealed truths to His disciples gradually, we must learn to handle what God gives us with discretion and humility. Another significant test of trust is your obedience and consistency. God tests whether you are a hearer and a doer of His Word. Can you be relied upon to follow His instructions, even when challenging, uncomfortable, or not immediately rewarding? Consistency over time builds trust. Just as in any relationship, being dependable in your walk with God strengthens the bond of trust. When God sees you consistently obedient, regardless of circumstances, He knows He can trust you with more significant things. Abraham's willingness to obey God, even to the point of offering his son Isaac, demonstrated his faithfulness and readiness for the fulfillment of God's promises.

Connecting with Those Who Know God's Secrets

While God reveals His secrets directly to specific individuals, He also calls us to connect with others who have a deep relationship with Him. These people have proven themselves trustworthy in God's eyes and carry valuable spiritual insights that can benefit your growth. Connecting with spiritual mentors is essential to growing in your faith and spiritual journey. These individuals, who have walked closely with God for many years, carry valuable insights and wisdom from experience. They are often entrusted with divine revelations and can offer guidance on how to walk in faith, obedience, and understanding.

Learning from such mentors can help you mature spiritually and navigate the challenges and revelations God brings into your life. Proverbs 13:20, *"Walk with the wise and become wise."* This principle encourages us to surround ourselves with people who are mature in their faith. These wise individuals can offer advice, encouragement, and insights from their personal experiences with God. By seeking out wise counsel, you allow yourself to grow and be shaped by those who have a deeper understanding of spiritual matters. Whether it's joining a small group, seeking mentorship from a pastor, or simply being in fellowship with others who are committed to God, surrounding yourself with wise and spiritually mature people helps you grow in your walk with God. Their experiences can serve as a guide for how to handle your challenges and revelations from God.

Just as Elisha followed and learned from Elijah (2 Kings 2:9), we are called to honor and learn from those whom God has placed in authority over us. These mentors—whether pastors, spiritual leaders, or elders—carry wisdom and divine secrets acquired through their faith journey. They have often been entrusted with insights into God's will and His ways, and their guidance can be invaluable in helping you grow spiritually. By honoring spiritual authority, you open yourself up to learn from their experiences and receive their wisdom. Their instruction can help you navigate your spiritual journey more effectively, understanding how to respond to God's calling and revelations. Spiritual mentors can help you avoid common pitfalls, guiding you toward deeper faith and obedience.

Spiritual relationships are essential for growth in faith, encouragement, and mutual accountability. Beyond learning from mentors, we are called to engage in meaningful, supportive relationships with fellow believers who seek to walk closely with God. These relationships help sharpen our faith, provide support during trials, and encourage us to focus on God's purposes. Proverbs 27:17, *"As iron sharpens iron, so one person sharpens another."*

When we connect with others serious about their faith, we challenge and encourage each other to grow. These relationships allow us to share our experiences, insights, and revelations from God, helping each other handle divine secrets with care and integrity. We strengthen our walk with God through open conversations, prayer, and mutual support. These spiritual connections act as a refining process, making us more effective in living out our faith and understanding the deeper truths of God. Building these relationships creates a space for accountability and helps us stay on track as we pursue spiritual maturity. Ephesians 4:16 speaks of the church as a body, saying, *"From him, the whole body, joined and held together by every supporting ligament, grows and builds itself up in love, as each part does its work."*

Spiritual relationships are beneficial for personal growth and the growth and unity of the church as a whole. God's revelations and secrets are often given not just to individuals but to the collective body of Christ. When we come together as a community, sharing the wisdom and insights God has revealed to each of us, we can fulfill His broader purposes on earth.

Unity within the church strengthens our witness and enables us to accomplish more for the kingdom of God. Spiritual growth happens best in a community where we can learn from each other, encourage one another, and build each other up in love. Whether through small groups, church gatherings, or one-on-one friendships, building these spiritual relationships allows us to stay focused on God's will and His work.

CHAPTER THREE

MASTERING SPIRITUAL PRINCIPLES

Mastery in the Christian life goes beyond the basics of faith and involves a deeper understanding of living out our beliefs daily. This mastery isn't just for personal gain but is meant to be shared with others through discipleship. As we grow in our walk with God, we are called not just to be learners but to become teachers, helping others along their spiritual journeys.

Signs of Spiritual Maturity
Spiritual maturity is not about how long you've been a Christian but about how deeply you've applied God's truth to your life. Spiritual maturity can be seen in your thoughts, actions, and the fruit you produce as a follower of Christ. A key indicator of spiritual maturity is obedience to God's Word. Spiritual maturity isn't just about knowing Scripture; it's about living it out daily. James 1:22, *"Do not merely listen to the word, and so deceive yourselves. Do what it says."*

True obedience means allowing God's Word to shape our decisions, behaviors, and attitudes. A mature believer moves beyond studying Scripture for knowledge and applying it practically. For example, Jesus teaches us in Matthew 5:44 to love our enemies and pray for those who persecute us. While this command might seem complicated, a mature Christian strives to live it out, showing love even in the hardest situations.

Obeying God's Word becomes most evident when it challenges us. It's easy to follow biblical principles when life goes smoothly, but true maturity is tested in difficult or inconvenient moments. A mature believer stands firm in faith, choosing to obey God's instructions even when it means making sacrifices, enduring hardships, or going against societal norms. This might mean telling the truth when lying seems easier or forgiving someone who has hurt you deeply.

Spiritual maturity also involves consistent obedience. It's not about obeying God only when it's convenient or we feel like it. Instead, it's about making obedience a daily habit, regardless of circumstances. As we continually align our thoughts, actions, and decisions with God's Word, we grow stronger in our faith and deepen our relationship with Him. When we live in obedience to God's Word, we position ourselves to receive His blessings. Deuteronomy 28:1-2 tells us that blessings will follow those who carefully obey God's commands. Obedience brings peace, joy, and purpose, as we walk in the plans God has laid out for us. It also helps us develop a deeper understanding of His will, allowing us to live more in line with His purpose.

Faithfulness during trials is a defining characteristic of a mature believer. Life is filled with challenges, but a mature Christian remains steadfast, trusting in God's faithfulness even when circumstances seem overwhelming. Romans 8:28 reassures us that *all things work together for good to those who love God, to those who are called according to His purpose.* This means that, no matter how difficult a situation may seem, God is actively working for our benefit and His greater plan. It's natural to question why God allows specific trials in our lives in times of hardship.

However, a spiritually mature person shifts from questioning to trusting. They believe that God's wisdom far surpasses human understanding and that He can see the bigger picture even when we cannot. Trusting in God's plan means that even when life doesn't make sense, we remain confident that He is guiding us toward His purpose. Spiritual maturity provides the strength to endure trials with patience and hope.

The Bible tells us that trials are not meaningless—they refine us and strengthen our faith. James 1:2-4, *"Consider it pure joy, my brothers and sisters, whenever you face trials of many kinds, because you know that the testing of your faith produces perseverance."* Through patience, we learn to wait on God's perfect timing, trusting that He will come through for us. On the other hand, hope keeps us looking forward to God's promises, knowing that our current struggles will eventually give way to His victory.

Mature believers can look beyond their immediate pain and recognize that God has a greater purpose for their trials. Just as Joseph endured betrayal, imprisonment, and hardship before rising to a place of prominence in Egypt (Genesis 50:20), we can trust that God is using our struggles for future good. Faithfulness in trials also involves surrendering control. We may not understand why God allows certain things to happen, but as mature believers, we surrender our need for immediate answers and trust that His plans are for our ultimate good.

A key to enduring trials faithfully is knowing that God never abandons us. He is with us every step of the way, providing comfort, strength, and peace. Psalm 46:1 declares, *"God is our refuge and strength, an ever-present help in trouble."* When we face difficult times, God stands with us, providing the grace to endure and the hope to keep moving forward.

In Galatians 5:22-23, the Apostle Paul describes the fruit of the Spirit as "love, joy, peace, patience, kindness, goodness, faithfulness, gentleness, and self-control." These are the qualities that the Holy Spirit produces in the lives of believers, and they serve as evidence of spiritual maturity.

Love is the foundational fruit. It reflects the unconditional love that God shows us and calls us to demonstrate toward others. A mature Christian loves selflessly, putting the needs of others above their own, as modeled by Christ. 1 Corinthians 13:4-7 describes love as patient, kind, and enduring, even under challenging circumstances. As we mature, we learn to love as Jesus loved, without expecting anything in return.

Joy is more than just happiness; it's a deep-seated gladness that comes from knowing God, regardless of circumstances. A mature believer enjoys the Lord and His promises, even when challenging. This joy is rooted in a relationship with God and is not dependent on external situations. Peace is the assurance that God is in control, even when life feels chaotic.

A mature Christian rests in this peace, trusting that God will guide and protect them. This peace keeps us centered in God's will, no matter what storms we face. Patience, or long-suffering, means having a calm endurance in the face of adversity. A mature Christian understands that God's timing is perfect, and they patiently wait on Him. Romans 12:12: *"Be patient in affliction, faithful in prayer."* This patience is also reflected in how we deal with others, offering grace and forgiveness as God does. Kindness is about showing compassion and generosity to others. It's an active expression of love.

A mature believer is kind when it's convenient and as a way of life, reflecting God's kindness toward us. Ephesians 4:32: "Be *kind to one another, tenderhearted, forgiving one another, as God in Christ forgave you."* Goodness speaks to living a life of integrity and doing what is right. A mature Christian seeks to reflect God's goodness by being honest, fair, and morally upright. Psalm 34:14: *"Depart from evil and do good; seek peace and pursue it."* Goodness flows from a heart that is aligned with God's righteousness.

Faithfulness is about being dependable, loyal, and trustworthy. A mature believer is faithful to God, consistently walking in

His ways and keeping His commandments. Gentleness involves humility and a soft, respectful approach toward others. A mature Christian is gentle, even when correcting or disagreeing with others, showing consideration and understanding. Self-control is the ability to govern our thoughts, emotions, and actions in alignment with God's will.

A mature believer exercises self-control in every area of life, resisting temptation and acting with discipline. 2 Timothy 1:7 says, *"God gave us a spirit not of fear but of power and love and self-control."* This fruit enables us to live in a way that honors God, even in the face of challenges. The fruit of the Spirit doesn't develop overnight. It's a process that takes time as we grow closer to God and allow the Holy Spirit to transform us. As we mature, these qualities become more evident in our daily lives, not because of our efforts but because we are yielding to the work of the Holy Spirit.

Another key indicator of spiritual maturity is a heart dedicated to serving others. Mature believers understand that their faith is not meant for personal benefit alone but to be shared and expressed through service. Jesus set the ultimate example of a servant's heart when He said in Matthew 20:28, *"The Son of Man came not to be served, but to serve, and to give His life as a ransom for many."* Accurate service comes from compassion and concern for others, reflecting Christ's love for humanity.

Mature believers are willing to put the needs of others ahead of their own, knowing that in serving others, they are ultimately serving God. Jesus emphasized the importance of helping the marginalized, saying, *"Whatever you did for one of the least of these brothers and sisters of mine, you did for me"* (Matthew 25:40). A mature believer recognizes the needs of those around them and responds with generosity, whether by providing physical help, emotional support, or spiritual encouragement. Service is not always about grand gestures. Sometimes, the most potent form of service is living as an example of Christ's love in everyday life.

Philippians 2:3-4 reminds us to *"do nothing out of selfish ambition or vain conceit. Rather, in humility, value others above yourselves, not looking to your interests but each of you to the interests of others."* By embodying humility, patience, and kindness, we can serve others by simply being a reflection of Christ's character. While service requires sacrifice, it also brings great joy. Acts 20:35 says, *"It is more blessed to give than to receive."* As we serve others, we experience the fulfillment of living out God's purpose. Mature believers enjoy seeing others blessed through service, knowing they play a part in God's kingdom work.

Discipleship: A Measure of Growth
After accepting the gift of salvation, discipleship becomes the next important step in our spiritual journey. Salvation is the foundation—it marks the beginning of a new life in Christ, where our sins are forgiven and reconciled with God. However, God's purpose for us extends beyond just being saved. He calls us to grow deeper in our relationship with Him by becoming disciples—committed followers of Jesus Christ who learn from His example and live according to His teachings.

Discipleship is about transformation and growth. It means moving from being a passive believer who has simply accepted Christ to becoming an active learner who constantly seeks to know more about God, His Word, and His ways.

Discipleship involves lifelong learning, improving, and being shaped by God through the Holy Spirit. It's not a one-time event but an ongoing journey where we grow in our faith and become more like Christ in our thoughts, actions, and character. When we commit to discipleship, we follow Jesus' example. Jesus didn't just tell people how to live; He showed them by the way He lived. His life was marked by love, compassion, humility, obedience to God, and service to others. As His disciples, we are called to follow His example by living out those same values. This means sacrificing our desires, taking up our cross daily (Luke 9:23), and serving others in love.

The process of discipleship is not something we do on our own. It's a partnership with the Holy Spirit, who guides, teaches, and helps us grow. As we walk in discipleship, the Holy Spirit works within us, transforming our hearts and minds to align more with God's will. Through prayer, studying Scripture, and being sensitive to the Spirit's leading, we allow God to shape us into the people He has called us to be.

In Matthew 28:19-20, Jesus gave the Great Commission to His followers: *"Go and make disciples of all nations, baptizing them in the name of the Father and of the Son and the Holy Spirit, and teaching them to obey everything I have commanded you."* This command goes beyond simply sharing the gospel—it emphasizes the importance of making disciples.

As disciples, we are called to follow Christ and help others grow in their faith. We are to teach them how to live according to God's principles, helping them become committed followers of Jesus. Discipleship is a lifelong commitment to spiritual growth. It requires dedication, persistence, and a willingness to be transformed by God. It's about becoming more Christ-like each day, allowing God to mold us through His Word and life's experiences. As we walk in discipleship, we will experience deeper intimacy with God, a greater understanding of His purpose for our lives, and the joy of helping others grow in their faith.

Discipleship demands serious commitment. It involves making significant sacrifices and prioritizing God's will over our desires and ambitions. Jesus Himself made this clear in Luke 9:23, saying, *"Whoever wants to be my disciple must deny themselves and take up their cross daily and follow me."*

Denying ourselves means letting go of personal desires, goals, and comforts that conflict with God's will. It's not about rejecting all pleasures or ambitions but aligning everything we do with God's purpose. For example, it may mean sacrificing time, resources, or relationships that distract us from our walk with God. It may also mean giving up pride or selfishness to live humbly and obey Christ's teachings. This self-denial can be difficult, especially in a world that often encourages us to prioritize our needs and desires. But discipleship calls for a different mindset, where we put God's will above all else.

When Jesus speaks of *"taking up our cross daily,"* He refers to the need for ongoing sacrifice and perseverance. In the time of Jesus, the cross symbolized suffering and sacrifice. Taking up our cross means being willing to endure challenges, trials, and even opposition to follow Christ. It's about being prepared to face difficulties with faith and trust in God. This also emphasizes that discipleship is a daily commitment. It's not something we do once and then forget about; instead, it is a continuous journey of following Christ and aligning our lives with His will. Each day presents new opportunities to trust God, make sacrifices, and choose His path over our own.

Although the cost of discipleship is high, the rewards far outweigh the sacrifices. By following Christ, we grow closer to God, experience His presence more deeply, and gain greater clarity about His purpose for our lives. We receive God's guidance, peace, and strength by walking obediently.

Additionally, discipleship allows us to become vessels of God's work on earth. When we live out our faith, we inspire others, and God uses us to lead people to salvation and spiritual growth. We become a part of God's more excellent plan, helping to build His kingdom and bring hope to others. Beyond the immediate rewards of a transformed life, discipleship also promises eternal rewards. Jesus assures us that following Him will lead to everlasting life and an inheritance in God's kingdom. In Matthew 16:25, Jesus said, "For whoever wants to save their life will lose it, but whoever loses their life for me will find it." This means that when we surrender our lives to Christ, we gain far more than we lose—both in this life and eternity.

One of the most precise indicators of spiritual growth is the ability to disciple others. Discipleship is not just something we receive— it's something we give. When we disciple others, we pass on the lessons God has taught us, helping others grow in their faith just as we have grown. Disciplining others is essential for the church's growth and continuing God's work on earth. Paul instructed Timothy to *"entrust to reliable people who will also be qualified to teach others"* (2 Timothy 2:2). This multiplication principle ensures that the gospel's message continues to spread, generation after generation. When we disciple others, we're helping to raise future leaders, teachers, and followers of Christ. We are passing on knowledge, and the wisdom and experience gained through our walk with God.

Disciplining others doesn't always mean formal teaching. Often, it happens through everyday interactions and relationships. When we invest in disciplining others, we create a ripple effect far beyond what we can see. The person we disciple today may go on to disciple others, who in turn will disciple more people. This is how the gospel spreads and how God's kingdom grows. By pouring into others, we become part of something much larger than ourselves—a movement that spans generations and transforms lives.

CHAPTER FOUR

THE PATH TO WINNING

A central goal in every believer's journey is to walk in victory with God. This chapter explores how we can claim God's promises, understand the relationship between divine guidance and life success, and recognize the importance of consistency in achieving lasting victory. God desires us to win, but this path requires active participation in His promises, aligning our lives with His purpose, and maintaining steadfast faithfulness. The Bible is filled with countless promises from God that speak of His goodness, protection, provision, and guidance.

However, it's not enough to simply know these promises— we must claim them through faith, obedience, and persistence. God's promises are unbreakable because they are rooted in His character. Numbers 23:19, *"God is not human, that he should lie, not a human being, that he should change his mind. Does he speak and then not act? Does he promise and not fulfill?"* He is faithful to keep it. Whether it's a promise of provision, healing, or guidance, we can trust that God will bring it to pass in His perfect timing. We must first stand on His promises with unwavering faith to win with God. This involves holding on to His Word, even when circumstances seem complicated or confusing.

The story of Abraham illustrates this well. In Genesis 18:16-19,

God promised Abraham about the future of his descendants and their role in God's plan. Though Abraham didn't immediately see the fulfillment of these promises, he continued to trust God's word. Even when life doesn't look like the promises are being fulfilled, faith is the substance that keeps us focused. Hebrews 11:1, *"Now faith is confidence in what we hope for and assurance about what we do not see."* This kind of faith believes God's Word regardless of the present situation.

The promises of God must be on our lips daily. Proverbs 18:21: *"The tongue has the power of life and death."* By speaking God's promises over our lives, we activate faith and align ourselves with His will. Claiming God's promises also involves obedience. James 2:17, *"Faith by itself, if it is not accompanied by action, is dead."* Obedience opens the door for God's promises to manifest in our lives. Abraham didn't just believe in God—he obeyed God's commands, even when they were brutal.

The Relationship Between God and Life Success
Many people desire success, but our relationship with God is the key to lasting success. True victory comes from walking closely with Him, following His guidance, and allowing His will to shape our lives. Success, in God's eyes, is more than material wealth or worldly achievements—it's living out our divine purpose, bearing fruit for His kingdom, and walking in His favor.

God's definition of success differs significantly from the world's view. While society often equates success with material wealth, fame, or power, God focuses on the heart, character, and the fulfillment of His divine purpose for our lives. In God's eyes, success is about obedience, faithfulness, and alignment with His will. Joshua 1:8 provides a clear blueprint for success according to God: *"Keep this Book of the Law always on your lips; meditate on it day and night, so that you may be careful to do everything written in it. Then you will be prosperous."* True success comes from living according to God's Word. It involves consistently meditating on Scripture, applying its teachings, and obeying God.

God's version of prosperity is not necessarily tied to material wealth but is more about spiritual growth, inner peace, and fulfilling His purposes. As we stay rooted in His Word and live according to His commands, we align ourselves with His plan, which brings true success. 1 Samuel 16:7: *"The Lord does not look at the things people look at. People look at the outward appearance, but the Lord looks at the heart."* God measures success based on our hearts' condition and willingness to follow Him. A heart that is humble, obedient, and committed to God's will is what He values. God's definition of success involves fulfilling His specific calling for each of us. This may not always align with worldly standards, but when we pursue His purpose for our lives, we experience a sense of peace, contentment, and spiritual prosperity.

Obedience to God's commandments is foundational to experiencing His favor and success. When we live according to His principles, we align ourselves with His purpose, which brings fulfillment and victory. Deuteronomy 28:1-2 promises blessings for those who faithfully follow God's commands: *"If you fully obey the Lord your God and carefully follow all His commands... all these blessings will come on you and accompany you."* In Matthew 6:33, *"But seek first His kingdom and righteousness, and all these things will be given to you as well."* When we put God first, trusting Him to provide for our needs, we position ourselves spiritually and daily for true success.

Success with God involves bearing spiritual fruit, as Jesus said in John 15:8: *"This is to my Father's glory, that you bear much fruit, showing yourselves to be my disciples."* Bearing fruit means living a life that reflects Christ's character—demonstrating love, joy, and peace and positively impacting others.

Fruitfulness is not just about personal achievements but about contributing to God's kingdom by helping others grow in their faith. Success in life is ultimately a result of God's favor and blessing, not just our efforts. Psalm 75:6-7 *"For promotion comes neither from the east, nor from the west, nor the south. But God is the judge: he puts down one and sets up another."* While hard work is essential, true success is determined by God's will. When we rely on Him as the source of all things, we recognize that every blessing and opportunity comes from His hand.

Trusting in God's timing and plan allows us to walk in a kind of victory that brings honor to Him, not just ourselves. Our dependence on Him for success keeps us grounded in humility and focused on His purpose for our lives. As Proverbs 16:3 says, *"Commit to the Lord whatever you do, and He will establish your plans."* When we place God at the center of our ambitions and rely on Him as our source, we are assured of success that aligns with His will and brings lasting fulfillment.

Consistency: A Key to Victory

One of the most critical keys to winning with God is consistency. Through daily, steady faithfulness, we build spiritual strength and gain victory. Many start well but fall short because they lack consistency in their walk with God. The journey to victory is not a sprint but a marathon that requires perseverance and commitment over time. Consistency matters because it demonstrates commitment and faithfulness. Just as an athlete must train regularly to achieve peak performance, believers must consistently pray, worship, and study God's Word to maintain spiritual strength. Luke 16:10 reminds us, *"Whoever can be trusted with very little can also be trusted with much."* God looks for consistent faithfulness in both small and large things. Consistency also involves enduring difficult times and persisting in faith even when things aren't easy. Hebrews 10:36, *"You need to persevere so that when you have done the will of God, you will receive what he has promised."* The road to victory often involves challenges, but those who remain steadfast and endure will see God's promises fulfilled.

Consistency is one of the most vital attributes for living a victorious life with God. Through regular devotion, obedience, and faithfulness, we grow spiritually and experience the fullness of God's promises. However, inconsistency is one of the greatest threats to that progress. This chapter explores the dangers of inconsistency, how to overcome challenges from the enemy and the importance of embracing a life of largeness and strength in Christ.

Spiritual consistency is about maintaining a steady, unwavering walk with God. It involves daily prayer, worship, obedience, and study of His Word, ensuring we don't waver in our relationship with Him. Many believers experience spiritual highs, but the actual test of maturity is maintaining that level of faithfulness over time, even when life gets tough.

Consistency is what transforms occasional spiritual experiences into a lasting relationship with God. It allows us to develop deep roots in our faith, making us more robust and resilient to our trials. Inconsistency, on the other hand, leaves us vulnerable to spiritual stagnation and the schemes of the enemy. Daniel's consistency in prayer, even in the face of danger, is an excellent example. He prayed three times a day, regardless of the challenges around him (Daniel 6:10). His commitment to God, even when threatened with death, showed his unwavering faith and trust in God's protection.

Jesus Himself demonstrated consistency in His relationship with the Father. Throughout His ministry, He often withdrew to pray and spend time alone with God (Luke 5:16). This consistent fellowship with the Father empowered Him to fulfill His divine mission.

The Impact of Inconsistency

Inconsistency in our spiritual life significantly hinders our growth and ability to experience God's fullness. Just as a plant requires regular care—consistent watering and sunlight —our souls need continuous nourishment through the Word of God, prayer, and obedience. Without this, we become spiritually malnourished, weak, and vulnerable. When we aren't consistently seeking Him, we may find it difficult to discern His voice and direction in our lives. Without a strong foundation built through consistent faith practices, we may waver in times of difficulty or uncertainty. Regular communion with God helps us stay aligned with His plan.

Inconsistency leads to confusion and a sense of being lost. God often calls for faithfulness and persistence. Without consistent obedience and trust, we miss experiencing His promises fully realized in our lives. Consistency helps us build a strong relationship with God, which enables spiritual growth and stability. Like a well-tended plant bears fruit, a life consistently focused on God will also bear spiritual fruit.

The enemy's strategy is often to exploit our inconsistencies. Satan finds opportunities to bring doubt, discouragement, and distractions when we waver in our faith. Satan is aware that inconsistent believers are more vulnerable to his tactics. He uses several common strategies to exploit this weakness, often targeting areas where we are least prepared.

Delaying spiritual practices such as prayer, Bible reading, or fellowship weakens our spiritual foundation. We become more susceptible to temptation and spiritual decline when we put off these essential disciplines. The enemy uses the busyness of life, worldly concerns, and entertainment to divert our attention from God. When we focus too much on these distractions, we lose sight of our spiritual priorities and drift away from our walk with God.

Satan often attacks during difficult seasons or when there's a delay in the fulfillment of God's promises. He whispers lies, causing us to lose hope, doubt God's plan, or even give up. 1 Peter 5:8 warns us to *"be sober-minded; be watchful. Your adversary, the devil, prowls around like a roaring lion, seeking someone to devour."* Living a life of spiritual consistency acts as armor, protecting us from these attacks and allowing us to stand firm against the enemy's schemes.

Staying consistent in our faith journey strengthens our defense, keeps us focused on God's truth, and enables us to resist the enemy's strategies. To overcome inconsistency and the challenges from the enemy, we need intentionality and discipline in our spiritual walk. Establish a daily prayer routine, Bible reading, and meditation on God's Word. This keeps you connected to God and strengthens your spiritual muscles.

Surround yourself with believers who can encourage and hold you accountable in your walk. Hebrews 10:25 urges us not to neglect meeting together for encouragement. Keep your focus on God and His Word. Philippians 4:8 advises us to think about actual, honorable, just, pure, lovely, and commendable things. This helps block out distractions and negativity that may derail your spiritual growth. Stay committed to God, even when facing difficulties. James 1:12 encourages us to persevere under trial, promising we will receive the crown of life that the Lord promised to those who love Him.

Embracing a Life of Largeness and Strength

A consistent spiritual life leads to largeness and strength, crucial for walking in victory with God. Largeness refers to giving God space to work mightily in your life, while strength is the spiritual fortitude to carry out His will. The largeness of spirit is about expanding our capacity to receive from God and respond to His leading. It requires living with an open heart and mind, willing to embrace whatever God desires to do in our lives and through us for the benefit of others. This spiritual enlargement allows us to operate in greater faith, love, and purpose. Psalm 18:35, *"You have given me the shield of your salvation, and your right hand supported me, and your gentleness made me great."* God's gentleness—His guidance and care—enables us to grow spiritually, positioning us for more incredible things. When we create space for God by removing barriers such as fear, doubt, or personal limitations, He enlarges our influence and impact. This means we are not only transformed internally but also equipped to make a significant difference in the lives of others. The largeness of spirit is about allowing God to move mightily in and through us, fulfilling His purpose on a grander scale. It's about trusting God to do great things and stepping out of your comfort zone to follow His lead.

The first step to living a significant life is surrendering to God's plan. This means being open to whatever God calls you to do, even if it feels challenging or beyond your abilities. Sometimes, we want to stick to what's comfortable or easy, but God often asks us to step out in faith. In 2 Corinthians 12:9-10, Paul reminds us that God's power works best when we are weak. It says, *"My grace is sufficient for you, for my power is made perfect in weakness."* When we surrender to God, we admit that we can't do everything independently, but we trust He will strengthen and guide us. God can do amazing things when we are willing to let go and let Him take control. Another way to live significantly is by thinking big. Don't limit God with small dreams or low expectations. God can do so much more than we can imagine, as Ephesians 3:20 says: *"Now to him who can do immeasurably more than all we ask or imagine."* Sometimes, we limit ourselves by thinking we're incapable of more, but God sees our potential that we may not see. God has great plans for your life and wants you to trust Him to do big things. Whether in your personal life, relationships, or career, God can exceed your expectations if you open your heart and mind to His possibilities. Living large also means living with a generous spirit. This involves sharing your time, resources, and gifts with others. When you give generously, God increases your capacity to bless more people. Proverbs 11:25, *"A generous person will prosper; whoever refreshes others will be refreshed."* When you pour into others, God pours more into you.

Generosity doesn't just mean giving money; it can be as simple as offering a helping hand, giving your time, or sharing your talents. When you live with an open hand, God blesses you and enlarges your life in ways you couldn't imagine. Living a significant life requires faith. You need to trust that God will provide for you and guide you every step of the way. Faith helps you move forward even when you can't see the whole picture. As you grow in faith, you also grow in your ability to live the significant life God has planned for you. Hebrews 11:6, *"Without faith, it is impossible to please God."* Faith is the foundation of everything in the Christian life. The more you trust God, the more He will show you how to live beyond your current circumstances. Largeness isn't about boasting or thinking highly of ourselves—it's about realizing that everything we have comes from God.

Staying humble means acknowledging that God is the source of our success and blessings. James 4:10, *"Humble yourselves before the Lord, and he will lift you."* When we live humbly, we allow God to lift us in His timing and for His purposes. Actual largeness comes from relying on God's strength and wisdom, not our own. Lastly, living a significant life requires persistence. There will be challenges along the way, but don't give up. Galatians 6:9 encourages us, "Let us not become weary in doing good, for at the proper time we will reap a harvest if we do not give up." Keep pushing forward, trusting God works even when you don't see immediate results. God has called us to live a life of largeness, not just for ourselves, but to make a difference in the world. When you surrender to God, think big, live generously, grow in faith, stay humble, and persist in your walk with Him, you'll see God move in mighty ways.

Building Spiritual Resilience
Spiritual resilience is the ability to bounce back from challenges and remain firm in your faith, even during difficult times. Just like physical strength is built through exercise, spiritual strength is developed through consistent discipline and trust in God. Isaiah 40:31 encourages us by saying, *"Those who wait for the Lord shall renew their strength; they shall mount up with wings like eagles; they shall run and not be weary; they shall walk and not faint."* When we depend on God and remain steady in our faith, He will empower

us to endure and thrive in all circumstances.

Reading the Bible is one of the most important ways to develop spiritual resilience. God's Word is full of promises, wisdom, and guidance that strengthen us. When we read and meditate on Scripture, we build a strong foundation for our faith. Prayer is our direct line of communication with God. It's where we can express our thoughts, feelings, and needs while seeking His guidance and strength. Regular prayer helps us stay connected to God and reminds us of His faithfulness.

Building resilience often requires patience. Waiting on the Lord doesn't mean being inactive; trusting He is working, even when we can't see it. Patience helps us endure challenges and grow in our faith. Having a solid support system is essential for building resilience. Surrounding yourself with fellow believers can encourage you in your faith and help you stay accountable. Sharing struggles and victories with others can strengthen your spiritual journey.

Difficult times can be tricky, but they also provide growth opportunities. Instead of viewing challenges as setbacks, try to see them as chances to develop strength and resilience in your faith. Gratitude can shift your focus from problems to the blessings in your life. Recognizing and appreciating what God has done for you builds resilience and strengthens your faith. God's promises are a source of strength and hope. When we trust in what He has promised, we can face difficulties with confidence.

Reminding ourselves of God's faithfulness can help us remain steadfast during trials. True strength comes from God, not our efforts. Philippians 4:13, *"I can do all things through Christ who strengthens me."* We must depend on His power, not our own, to face challenges. Spiritual strength grows through enduring hardship. James 1:3-4 teaches that testing our faith produces perseverance, which leads to spiritual maturity and strength. Strength is developed as we put our faith into action. Just as physical strength grows through exercise, our spiritual strength increases as we step out in faith, trust God in uncertainty, and obey His commands, even when difficult.

CHAPTER FIVE

GOD'S PERSPECTIVE ON YOUR FUTURE

God sees beyond your present struggles, limitations, and even your self-perception. While you might see weaknesses, failures, or limitations, God sees potential, strength, and a purpose yet to unfold. His perspective is eternal and all-encompassing, viewing your life from the beginning to the end with complete clarity. Jeremiah 1:5, "Before I formed you in the womb I knew you, before you were born I set you apart; I appointed you as a prophet to the nations."

God's knowledge of us is not confined to our physical birth but extends to His eternal design for our lives. He knows the gifts, talents, and calling placed within each of us long before we are even aware of them. God's perspective is perfect and complete. While we might see ourselves as incapable or unworthy, God sees us through His grace and divine purpose. When Gideon saw himself as the least in his family and tribe, God saw a *"mighty warrior"* (Judges 6:12).

God's vision for your life encompasses your current situation and the person you are becoming as you walk in faith and obedience. God doesn't just see who you are today; He sees the person you will become as you mature in Him. His goal is to mold and shape you into the image of Christ (Romans 8:29). Spiritual growth and maturity are part of His long-term plan for every believer. Philippians 1:6, *"being confident of this, that He who began a good work in you will carry it on to completion until the day of Christ Jesus."*

God's vision is one of continual transformation. He sees your trials as opportunities for growth, your weaknesses as avenues for His strength, and your failures as learning moments. From His perspective, each challenge is a stepping stone toward fulfilling your calling.

The Importance of God's Vision

A clear vision of God is essential for living a meaningful and fulfilling life. God's vision helps us understand His plans, guides our decisions, and gives us hope. God's vision acts like a map showing us where to go. It helps us make decisions that align with His plans and purpose. If you feel called to help others, you might choose a career in healthcare, social work, or ministry. God's vision for your life guides this decision. When faced with choices, ask yourself, "Does this fit with what I believe God wants for me?" This keeps you on the right path.

God's vision provides a sense of purpose. It reminds us that our lives have meaning and that we are part of something bigger than ourselves. When you know that God has a plan for your life, you wake up daily with excitement and purpose. You understand that your actions matter and can make a difference. Having a purpose helps us stay focused and motivated, especially during difficult times. Life can be tricky, and challenges may come our way.

God's vision gives us hope, reminding us that He is in control and has a plan for our future. This hope helps us endure hardships and keeps us from losing faith. God's vision often pushes us to grow and change. It encourages us to step out of our comfort zones and become who He created us to be. Embracing change allows us to discover our strengths and potential. When we follow God's vision together as a community or church, it brings unity and cooperation. We can work together towards a common goal.

Working together fosters solid relationships and encourages teamwork, making a more significant impact than we could achieve alone. Trusting in God's vision builds our faith. Our trust in Him grows stronger when we see how He guides us and fulfills His promises. Reflecting on how God has led you in the past helps you trust Him for the future. You may remember uncertain times, but God provided what you needed.

Trusting God leads to deeper faith and reliance on Him in every aspect of our lives. Living out God's vision can inspire others to seek His purpose in their own lives. When people see your faith and how you follow God's guidance, they may be encouraged to do the same. Your actions can serve as a testimony to others, leading them to discover God's vision for themselves.

Aligning Yourself with God's Vision

Proverbs 29:18, *"Where there is no vision, the people perish."* When you align yourself with God's vision, you are not easily swayed by distractions or discouragement. His vision anchors your faith, helping you to stay focused on the bigger picture, even when circumstances seem difficult.

Aligning with God's vision requires surrendering your limited understanding and trusting He knows what is best. Isaiah 55:8-9 reminds us that God's ways and thoughts are higher than ours. Even when it doesn't make sense now, trusting in His plan is essential for fulfilling your destiny. Without a vision, we can quickly lose our way and become distracted by life's challenges. When we align ourselves with God's vision, we are better equipped to stay focused on His plans, even during tough times.

Aligning yourself with God's vision is about understanding His plans for your life and making choices that reflect those plans. It means being open to His guidance and trusting He knows what is best for you. Prayer is a vital way to communicate with God. It helps you understand His heart and His plans for you. When you pray, you invite God into your decision-making process. It enables you to gain clarity and direction. The Bible is filled with wisdom and guidance. Reading and reflecting on Scripture helps you understand God's character and plans for you. God's Word is a lamp to our feet (Psalm 119:105). It illuminates our path and helps us align our lives with His vision.

Aligning with God's vision often requires changing our plans or attitudes. Being open to His leading means stepping out of your comfort zone. When you feel a nudge from God to try something new or let go of something old, take a moment to pray about it. Ask for courage to make the necessary changes. God often calls us to grow and stretch beyond our current abilities.

Embracing change allows us to become who He wants us to be. God speaks in many ways—through His Word, prayer, circumstances, and the wisdom of others. Paying attention to these can help you understand His vision. Listening is essential for discerning God's voice. It enables you to align your actions with His will. Surrounding yourself with spiritually mature people can provide valuable insights and encouragement. Wise counsel can help you see things from a different angle and confirm what you believe God is saying to you.

Once you feel aligned with God's vision, take steps to put your faith into action. Faith is not just about believing; it's about doing. Identify specific actions that align with God's vision for your life. It could be volunteering, pursuing education, or being kind to others. Taking action shows your commitment to following God's vision. It also allows you to experience the joy of seeing His plans unfold.

God speaks to us in various ways, helping us understand His will and guiding us through life. The Bible is God's primary way of talking to us. It contains His truths, promises, and guidance for our lives. When you read the Bible, God can speak directly to your heart through the verses. You may find comfort, direction, or correction in the words you read. 2 Timothy 3:16-17 tells us that all Scripture is inspired by God and useful for teaching, rebuking, correcting, and training in righteousness.

Prayer is our way of talking to God. It creates two-way communication where we can share our hearts and listen to His response. When you pray, take time to listen quietly afterward. God may bring thoughts, feelings, or ideas to your mind that guide you. Philippians 4:6-7 encourages us to present our requests to God and promises His peace will guard our hearts and minds.

The Holy Spirit is our helper and guide. He lives within believers and helps us understand God's will. The Holy Spirit can prompt you with thoughts, feelings, or convictions. These can be reminders of God's Word or nudges toward a particular action. John 14:26 says the Holy Spirit will teach us everything and remind us of what Jesus said.

God can use the events in our lives to guide us. This includes both challenges and blessings. Sometimes, doors will open or close, directing you toward or away from specific paths. Pay attention to the situations around you. God often speaks to us through others —friends, family, pastors, or mentors. They can offer insights and encouragement. Wise counsel from other believers can help confirm what God is saying. It can be through advice, teaching, or even a simple word of encouragement.

God speaks through the beauty of nature and the world around us. The wonders of creation reveal His character and power. Observing the beauty and complexity of nature can lead to a sense of awe and understanding of God's greatness. It can remind you of His care and creativity.

Sometimes, God uses dreams or visions to communicate His messages. This is less common but can still happen. You may receive a clear message or insight while dreaming. If you believe a dream is from God, praying for understanding and confirmation is essential. Joel 2:28 says that God will pour out His Spirit and that people will prophesy, dream, and see visions.

Trusting God's Timing

Understanding that His perspective includes what will happen and when can help us navigate the uncertainties and delays we may face. Ecclesiastes 3:11, *"He has made everything beautiful in its time."* There is a right time for everything in our lives. While we may desire immediate results, God sees the bigger picture and knows the perfect timing for His plans. Think about planting a seed. You cannot expect to see a flower bloom the next day. It needs time to grow, be nurtured, and develop.

Similarly, God may prepare something beautiful in your life, but it requires patience and trust. Delays often frustrate us; we might interpret them as signs of failure or lack of progress. However, it's essential to understand that delays are not denials. Instead, they are often periods of growth and preparation. During waiting periods, God works on our character, teaching us patience, resilience, and faith. These qualities are crucial for the more significant plans He has for us.

Consider a caterpillar waiting to become a butterfly. It may not develop the strength to fly if it rushes out of the cocoon before it's ready. In the same way, we may need to grow stronger before stepping into our next season. Trusting God's timing means believing He knows what is best for us. It can be challenging, especially when we see others receiving their blessings.

Instead of comparing ourselves to others, we should focus on our journey with God. He has a unique path designed just for us. Abraham and Sarah waited many years for the birth of their son, Isaac. Despite their doubts, God's promise came at the right time (Genesis 21:1-2). Joseph after being sold into slavery and imprisoned, Joseph waited many years before he became the second-in-command in Egypt. His trials prepared him for the leadership role he was destined for (Genesis 41:46). When we trust God's timing, we can rest assured that He is faithful. He will fulfill His promises and plans for us, often in ways that exceed our expectations. Jeremiah 29:11, *"For I know the plans I have for you," says the Lord. "Plans to prosper you and not to harm you plans to give you hope and a future."* Your attitude plays a significant role in navigating your journey toward fulfilling God's vision for your life. While God has a perfect plan for us, our willingness to cooperate with that plan and develop the right mindset determines how we experience His promises.

Negative attitudes like fear, doubt, procrastination, and discouragement can derail your journey. The Israelites failed to enter the Promised Land due to their fear and unbelief, despite God's promise (Numbers 14:1-4). Their attitude prevented them from experiencing the fullness of God's plan. Cultivating an attitude of trust, hope, and perseverance is essential. Romans 12:2 reminds us to "be transformed by renewing your mind." This transformation requires replacing negative thoughts with God's truth, holding on to His promises, and maintaining a hopeful outlook, even in difficult situations.

CHAPTER SIX

THE SPIRIT OF GENEROSITY

G enerosity is one of the most beautiful expressions of the heart. It reflects God's nature and character, showing how much He cares for His creation. Generosity is about the heart. It is a mindset and attitude that recognizes the abundance of God's blessings and the desire to share those blessings with others.

A generous heart is open, compassionate, and willing to extend kindness to those in need. True generosity goes beyond giving money or material possessions. It involves a genuine desire to help others and to make a positive impact on their lives. Proverbs 11:25 says, *"A generous person will prosper; whoever refreshes others will be refreshed."* When we give to others, we are also blessed in return.

Generosity begins with gratitude. When we recognize all God has done for us, we naturally want to share those blessings. In 2 Corinthians 9:8, *"And God can bless you abundantly, so that in all things at all times, having all that you need, you will abound in every good work."* Understanding that we are stewards of God's gifts helps us embrace a spirit of generosity. A generous heart is not only beneficial to those who receive but also to the giver. It fosters community and connection, creating bonds between individuals and within communities.

Generosity breaks down barriers and creates opportunities for collaboration and mutual support. It cultivates empathy and compassion, allowing us to see the world through the eyes of others. A generous heart reflects the character of Christ. Jesus exemplified ultimate generosity by giving His life for our salvation. As His followers, we are called to emulate His generosity in our own lives. When we embrace a generous heart, we mirror His love and compassion to the world around us.

Property Giving Beyond Measure: Intellectual and Gifts

Generosity is often thought of as giving money or material possessions. However, it is much broader than that. True generosity includes sharing our intellectual property and unique gifts with others. This can involve our knowledge, skills, talents, and experiences, invaluable resources that can positively impact those around us. In today's world, sharing knowledge is a powerful way to impact lives. Whether through mentoring, teaching, or simply offering guidance, sharing what you know can open doors for others. For instance, if you have expertise in a specific field, consider mentoring someone just starting. Your insights and experiences can help them navigate challenges and grow in their journey. Proverbs 1:5 *"Let the wise listen and add to their learning, and let the discerning get guidance."* We empower others and contribute to their growth and success by sharing our knowledge.

Everyone is gifted with unique arts, writing, music, or problem-solving talents. Sharing these talents can uplift others and inspire them to pursue their passions. For example, a musician can organize free workshops for aspiring artists, or a writer can share their experiences and tips with budding authors. When we give of ourselves, we create opportunities for others to grow and flourish. In Matthew 25:29, *"To those who use well what they are given, even more will be given, and they will have an abundance."* By investing our gifts in others, we create a ripple effect of generosity that can transform lives. Becoming a mentor allows you to guide someone in their personal or professional journey. By sharing your experiences and knowledge, you help them navigate challenges and seize opportunities.

Everyone has talents in art, music, writing, or sports. These gifts can inspire, uplift, and encourage others. Use your abilities to serve your community. For example, musicians can perform at local events, artists can create murals or public art, and writers can share uplifting stories or resources. Our life experiences—challenges and triumphs—are powerful tools for helping others. When we share our stories, we offer hope and encouragement to those facing similar situations. Sharing your journey can inspire others to overcome their obstacles. When we give beyond measure—sharing our knowledge, skills, talents, and experiences—we create a ripple effect of positivity and growth.

Generosity fosters more profound connections with others. We develop bonds built on trust, respect, and mutual support when we share our gifts. The Bible encourages us to be generous with our gifts and talents. In 1 Peter 4:10, *"Each of you should use whatever gift you have received to serve others, as faithful stewards of God's grace in its various forms."* Our abilities are not just for our benefit but are meant to serve and uplift others.

When we embody a spirit of generosity and share our resources, knowledge, and gifts, we can significantly contribute to the world around us. These contributions can potentially create lasting change and positively impact future generations.

Generosity can manifest in various forms, such as volunteering, supporting local charities, or starting initiatives that address community needs. When we recognize the challenges those around us face, we can take action to alleviate their struggles. Acts of kindness and service can inspire others to join in, creating a culture of generosity and support. Our actions, fueled by generosity, can bring hope and inspiration to those who may feel lost or marginalized.

The spirit of generosity can extend beyond our immediate communities and create a global impact. Initiatives such as supporting mission trips, donating to international relief efforts, or advocating for social justice can help address pressing issues worldwide. By sharing our resources and voices, we can contribute to meaningful change on a larger scale.

The story of the Good Samaritan (Luke 10:25-37) exemplifies how one act of kindness can create a lasting impact. The Samaritan's compassion for the injured man changed not only that man's life but also served as an enduring lesson for all of us about the importance of helping others in need, regardless of their background or circumstances.

Our contributions can leave a legacy of generosity for future generations. By modeling a generous spirit, we inspire others to follow suit and create a cycle of giving that transcends time. This legacy can take many forms, from building foundations and scholarships to simply instilling the values of kindness and compassion in the next generation. Acts 20:35, *"It is more blessed to give than to receive."* This truth reinforces that the impact of our generosity reaches far beyond our individual lives; it has the potential to shape communities, cultures, and even nations.

CHAPTER SEVEN

THE IMPACT OF
OUR ACTIONS

Our presence in the world matters. Each one of us carries the ability to influence our surroundings and the people within them. This influence can be positive or negative, depending on our choices and actions. People often learn and grow by observing others. As individuals committed to living out God's principles, we can be role models in our communities, workplaces, and families.

How we conduct ourselves can inspire others to do the same, fostering a culture of kindness, respect, and integrity. Matthew 5:14-16, *"You are the light of the world. A town built on a hill cannot be hidden. Neither do people light a lamp and put it under a bowl. Instead, they put it on its stand, giving everyone in the house light."* Our actions serve as a light, guiding others toward truth and goodness.

Every action can create a ripple effect, impacting many lives beyond our immediate circle. A simple act of kindness, a word of encouragement, or a helping hand can spark positivity in others, prompting them to pay it forward. For instance, if we help a neighbor, they might be inspired to assist someone in need. This chain reaction can spread hope and love throughout our communities.

Conversely, negative actions can also have far-reaching consequences. Gossip, negativity, or unkind behavior can create a toxic atmosphere that breeds distrust and resentment. We must be mindful of how our presence can affect others, choosing actions that foster unity and uplift those around us.

Living with Integrity and Purpose

Living with integrity means aligning our actions with our values and beliefs. Committing to being honest and transparent creates a foundation of trust in our relationships and communities. Integrity is a fundamental quality that defines who we are. It involves doing what is right, even when no one is watching. This means being true to ourselves and holding ourselves accountable for our actions, regardless of external pressure or temptation.

Integrity is more than just honesty; it encompasses our entire character. It means aligning our actions with our values and principles. When we act with integrity, we make choices that reflect our beliefs and morals, allowing us to live authentically. Integrity requires us to be consistent in our behavior and decisions. This means we act the same way in all situations, whether in public or private.

Living with integrity means being genuine. It involves being true to ourselves and not pretending to be someone we are not. The Bible places great importance on integrity. Proverbs 11:3, *"The integrity of the upright guides them, but the crookedness of the treacherous destroys them."* When we act with integrity, we navigate life with clarity and purpose. Integrity builds trust with others. When people know they can rely on us to act honestly and fairly, they feel safe and secure in their relationships. Acting with integrity aligns us with God's will.

In Psalm 25:21, we see a prayer for integrity and uprightness, showing that these qualities are valued in our relationship with God. Living with integrity has numerous benefits, not just for ourselves but for those around us. When we act with integrity, we can rest easy knowing we are making the right choices. This brings inner peace and confidence in our decisions. Integrity fosters strong, trusting relationships.

When honest and transparent with others, we build a foundation of respect and loyalty. People respect those who act with integrity. A reputation for honesty and fairness opens doors for opportunities and collaborations. Commit to being truthful in all situations, even when it is difficult. This includes owning up to mistakes and being transparent in your dealings with others.

Regularly reflect on your core values and ensure your actions align with them. This will guide your decisions and help you remain steadfast in your integrity. We may feel tempted to compromise our values to fit in or gain approval from others. It's essential to stand firm in our beliefs, even when uncomfortable. Sometimes, doing the right thing can have negative consequences, such as losing a job or facing criticism. Remember that the long-term benefits of integrity far outweigh the temporary discomfort.

Living purposefully is about understanding our God-given mission and working to fulfill it daily. We are created with unique gifts, talents, and callings that play a part in the greater good. The Bible reminds us of this truth in Ephesians 2:10: *"For we are God's handiwork, created in Christ Jesus to do good works, which God prepared in advance for us to do."* When we live with intention and focus on our purpose, we become powerful instruments of change and healing in our world. Purpose is more than just having goals; it's about knowing why we exist and what we are meant to do. It gives direction to our lives and influences our choices.

Understanding our purpose can help us find joy and fulfillment, even in difficult times. Each person has been designed with a specific purpose. This means you are unique and significant in God's plan. God has created us not just to exist but to do good works that positively impact others. These works can take many forms, from serving in our communities to being a source of encouragement for friends and family. To live purpose-driven lives, we must actively seek to fulfill our God-given mission. When we know our purpose, making decisions that align with our values and contribute to our mission becomes more accessible. This clarity allows us to prioritize our time and energy on actions that matter.

Living with purpose benefits you and positively affects those around you. You inspire others to do the same when you live out your purpose. Your actions can encourage those around you to discover their missions. Purpose-driven individuals contribute to the greater good, fostering change and healing in their communities. Your unique gifts can address needs and make a lasting impact. Living with purpose brings a sense of fulfillment and joy. Life becomes more prosperous and meaningful when you know you contribute to something greater than yourself.

The Consequences of Our Choices

Every choice we make has consequences, both immediate and long-term. Understanding the weight of our decisions can help us make wiser choices that align with our goals and values. Our choices significantly impact our lives and shape who we are as individuals. The Bible reminds us of this truth in Galatians 6:7, *"Do not be deceived: God cannot be mocked. A man reaps what he sows."* This principle of sowing and reaping highlights that our actions carry consequences, and we will ultimately experience the results of our decisions. The choices we make are like seeds planted in the ground. When we act kindly, honestly, and compassionately, we sow good seeds that can grow into positive outcomes. These good actions can lead to fruitful relationships, personal growth, and fulfillment. Just as a farmer reaps what he has sown, we also experience the results of our actions. If we act selfishly, deceitfully, or negatively, we may face regret, broken relationships, and missed opportunities. The consequences of our choices can impact us and those around us.

Our character is formed through our choices. When we

consistently do what is right, our character strengthens and aligns more with God's values. Choosing honesty and integrity strengthens our character. When we make decisions that reflect our values, we build a reputation of trustworthiness, which can open doors for future opportunities.

Acts of kindness not only benefit others but also shape us into more compassionate individuals. When we help and uplift others, we become more empathetic and caring, which enriches our relationships. We all make poor choices at times. However, acknowledging our mistakes and learning from them helps us grow. When we take responsibility for our actions, we build resilience and wisdom. While making good choices leads to positive outcomes, poor decisions can have negative consequences. Poor choices often lead to feelings of regret. When we act selfishly or harm others, we may wish we had made different decisions. Regret can linger and affect our self-esteem and relationships.

Decisions rooted in negativity or dishonesty can damage our relationships with family, friends, and colleagues. Once trust is broken, rebuilding can be challenging, leading to loneliness and isolation. When we make choices based on fear or insecurity, we may miss valuable opportunities for growth and success. Embracing risks and making bold choices can lead to new experiences and possibilities. Before making a decision, take a moment to think about the potential outcomes. Will this choice align with your values? How will it affect you and those around you? Making positive choices leads to a fulfilling life filled with joy, peace, and purpose. We can reflect on our lives satisfactorily, knowing we acted with integrity and kindness. Positive choices foster healthy relationships built on trust and respect. We cultivate deeper connections and a supportive community as we treat others well. Our choices can inspire others to make positive decisions as well. Leading by example creates a ripple effect that encourages those around us to choose wisely. While some consequences may be challenging, they can also be valuable lessons. When we make mistakes or experience the repercussions of our actions, it's an opportunity for growth. Reflecting on our choices allows us to understand their impact and adjust our behavior moving forward.

CHAPTER EIGHT

TRAINING THE NEXT GENERATION

Mentorship is a powerful tool for growth and development. It involves guiding, supporting, and inspiring individuals as they navigate their paths. A mentor's impact can be profound, influencing personal and professional choices and spiritual growth.

Mentors play a crucial role in providing guidance based on their experiences. They offer insights into navigating challenges, making decisions, and overcoming obstacles. Just as Paul mentored Timothy in the Bible, we are called to invest in the lives of others, sharing our wisdom and helping them grow in their faith and understanding. 2 Timothy 2:2, *"And the things you have heard me say in the presence of many witnesses entrust to reliable people who will also be qualified to teach others."*

A strong mentor-mentee relationship fosters a safe space for learning and growth. Mentors provide encouragement, challenge their mentees to reach their potential, and hold them accountable for their goals. This supportive environment helps individuals feel valued and understood, allowing them to flourish.

Learning at Every Stage of Life
Life is a continuous learning journey; embracing this process at every stage is essential. Regardless of age or experience,

there are always opportunities for growth and understanding. Lifelong learning is the ongoing, voluntary pursuit of knowledge throughout life. It's not limited to school or formal education but involves seeking growth in all areas—spiritually, mentally, and emotionally. Proverbs 1:5, *"Let the wise hear and increase in learning, and the one who understands obtain guidance."* This learning reminds us that there is always room to grow. Whether through reading, studying the Bible, attending workshops, or learning from life experiences, we should never stop growing. Each day provides new opportunities to gain wisdom and insight.

The world is constantly changing, and as followers of Christ, it's essential to adapt and respond wisely. Lifelong learning equips us to face new challenges with confidence. We can respond to life's ups and downs with grace and understanding by continually learning. For Christians, learning is about gaining worldly knowledge and deepening our understanding of God and His Word.

Life itself is an influential teacher. Through good and challenging times, God teaches us important lessons about trust, patience, and perseverance. We gain valuable insights from every season when we approach life with a learner's heart. As we grow in knowledge and experience, sharing with others becomes part of the learning process. Explaining a concept or sharing an experience strengthens your understanding.

Teaching others allows you to process information in new ways, which helps solidify what you've learned. By sharing your knowledge, you can inspire others to learn and grow. Whether teaching a Bible study, mentoring someone, or simply offering advice, your willingness to share can encourage others to pursue their learning journey.

While we may have a wealth of knowledge and experience to share, we must recognize the unique insights and fresh perspectives the younger generation offers. They see the world differently, shaped by new technologies, ideas, and cultural shifts. Engaging with their thoughts and experiences can expand our understanding and help bridge generational gaps.

Mutual learning fosters a relationship of respect and understanding. Opening ourselves to learn from the younger generation promotes a culture of collaboration where both sides benefit. The younger generation often sees solutions to problems in creative ways that older generations might not have considered. Their experiences, especially in a rapidly changing world, offer innovative ideas and approaches to enhance our understanding and problem-solving.

Learning from the younger generation helps break down stereotypes and assumptions between different age groups. It creates an atmosphere of mutual respect and shows that wisdom isn't limited to age but comes from a willingness to learn from everyone. Ecclesiastes 4:9-10, *"Two are better than one because they have a good reward for their toil. For if they fall, one will lift his fellow."* This verse reminds us of the strength found in working together.

Collaboration between generations leads to better outcomes for all. While older generations often act as mentors, guiding the younger ones, reverse mentorship allows younger people to teach their elders new skills or viewpoints. By fostering an environment where learning flows both ways, we cultivate growth for both young and old. The more we collaborate and share our knowledge and experiences, the stronger we become as individuals and communities. Engaging with younger people requires us to listen to their experiences and respect their ideas, even when they differ from ours. Younger generations often bring a passion for innovation and a drive for change that can positively influence how we approach problems. The openness and creativity that come naturally to many young people can inspire us to think differently about challenges. This creativity is a powerful tool that can bring fresh solutions to old problems. Jesus often engaged with people of all ages and backgrounds, showing us that learning and teaching are lifelong practices. He spent time with children and valued their faith, reminding us to approach learning with humility and openness.

Investing in Future Leaders

As mentors and leaders, we must recognize the unique strengths, talents, and abilities of those we guide. This is especially important when working with young people, as they often have untapped potential waiting to be developed. By helping them discover their passions and refining their skills, we empower them to pursue their dreams and step confidently into the future God has prepared for them. Each person has specific strengths and talents that set them apart.

A mentor's role is to recognize these gifts and help guide the person toward using them in a way that honors God and benefits others. Often, young people may not even realize the gifts they have. It is crucial to observe their interests, abilities, and passions. This might include their natural leadership skills, artistic talents, communication abilities, or empathy toward others. They can use these gifts more effectively when we help them see them. Once we identify their strengths, it's essential to help them nurture and refine these abilities.

Encouraging continuous learning, practice, and patience will help them develop their skills and confidence. As mentors, we can provide opportunities for them to use their gifts in real-life situations, offering constructive feedback and support. When we invest our time and energy into young people's growth, we help them realize their full potential.

Mentors act as guides, offering wisdom, experience, and encouragement that can significantly impact their lives. Many young people may feel unsure about their abilities or question whether they can make a difference. By consistently affirming their strengths and providing opportunities to step out of their comfort zone, we help them build the confidence to pursue their dreams.

Leadership is not always about position or power. It's about influencing others positively, leading by example, and using one's gifts for the greater good. By encouraging young people to step into leadership roles, we allow them to experience the responsibility and fulfillment of guiding others.

Mentorship is an investment in the future. The time, resources, and support we offer can shape not only the individual's life but also the lives of those they will influence. As young people grow and develop, they, in turn, will mentor others, creating a ripple effect of growth and leadership.

Mentoring requires a personal commitment. By dedicating time to walk alongside those we guide, we provide a foundation for their success. This investment can have long-term effects, shaping their lives' trajectory and helping them live out their God-given purpose. When we help young people step into their potential, we create a legacy of leadership. They become examples for others to follow, and their success in fulfilling their purpose is a testimony of what happens when talents are identified and nurtured. Youth is not a limitation. Young people are capable of outstanding leadership, influence, and wisdom. Paul's words to Timothy remind us that age does not define one's ability to make a difference. We should encourage young leaders to be confident and lead by example. While young leaders may have the passion and drive, they still need support and guidance. Mentors can provide the wisdom and experience that young leaders may not yet have, offering advice and encouragement as they navigate their leadership journey. To help young people realize their potential, creating opportunities to stretch themselves, take on responsibility, and grow is essential. These experiences help them apply their knowledge and develop resilience, problem-solving skills, and a sense of purpose.

Allowing young people to participate in real-life projects or leadership roles provides hands-on experience that builds confidence and capability. These opportunities show them they are trusted and capable of handling responsibilities, further encouraging their growth. Mentors should also create a safe and supportive environment where mistakes are seen as part of the learning process. This helps young people feel more secure in taking risks, knowing they are backed by someone who believes in their potential.

To truly invest in the next generation of leaders, we must provide them opportunities to grow, learn, and practice leadership. Creating environments where young people can take responsibility and develop their skills is crucial for their success. Establishing formal mentorship programs can have a lasting impact. These programs pair young individuals with experienced mentors who can guide them in their personal, spiritual, and professional growth.

A mentor can provide one-on-one support, offer advice, and share life experiences to help young leaders make wise decisions. Mentorship encourages accountability, as mentees have someone who supports their growth and helps them stay focused on their goals.

Mentors help younger individuals deepen their faith, providing biblical wisdom and prayer support. Leadership is not only about natural ability but also about skills that can be learned and refined. Offering training sessions or workshops can help young people sharpen these abilities.

Training should also emphasize the importance of teamwork and the ability to work well with others, fostering a collaborative spirit that enhances their leadership capacity. For Christian youth, integrating spiritual leadership training based on biblical principles can help them lead in both their faith communities and their personal lives.

For example, understanding servant leadership as Jesus taught can empower them to lead with humility and love. Encouraging young people to get involved in volunteer work is a powerful way to develop leadership qualities while serving others. This can be done through church activities, community service, or local outreach programs.

Volunteering provides hands-on leadership experience. Young people can lead teams, organize events, and take on roles that develop their planning, coordination, and leadership abilities. Volunteering also fosters compassion and empathy, which are essential for effective leadership. As they serve others, young leaders learn the importance of caring for those in need and putting others before themselves.

Volunteer roles give young people real responsibility, teaching them to manage tasks, work with others, and develop problem-solving skills.

Allowing young people to take initiative is an essential part of leadership development. Allowing them to take on projects or lead initiatives provides space for growth and learning. Assign young leaders specific projects where they can exercise creativity and responsibility. This helps them learn to lead and manage tasks while building confidence. When young people take on leadership roles, they face challenges that help them develop problem-solving skills.

Learning from these challenges helps them grow and become more resilient. Creating a supportive environment where young leaders can learn from mistakes without fear of failure is essential. By reflecting on these experiences, they can grow stronger and more capable. Young leaders thrive in environments where they feel supported and valued.

As mentors, teachers, or leaders, creating a nurturing space where they can take risks, make mistakes, and grow is vital. Positive reinforcement and celebrating their successes build confidence and motivate young leaders to continue growing. Providing gentle and constructive feedback helps young leaders learn and improve without feeling discouraged. They need to know that growth is a process and that every experience contributes to their development. For Christian youth, prayer is a foundational part of their leadership journey. Encouraging them to seek God's guidance and direction will help them lead with purpose and humility.

CHAPTER NINE

EMBRACING
IMPERFECTIONS

Mistakes are an inevitable part of life. We have made errors, whether in judgment, action, or communication. Instead of viewing mistakes as failures, we should see them as opportunities for growth and learning. When we make mistakes, we must reflect on what went wrong and why. This reflection helps us gain insight into our choices and actions, allowing us to identify areas for improvement. For example, Peter, one of Jesus' closest disciples, denied knowing Him three times. Despite this mistake, Peter grew from the experience, becoming a foundational leader in the early church. His story reminds us that our errors can lead to significant growth if we learn from them. Proverbs 24:16 says, "For though the righteous fall seven times, they rise again." We create a culture of acceptance and understanding when we embrace our imperfections. In our families, workplaces, and communities, we can encourage open dialogue about mistakes, fostering an environment where individuals feel safe to share their challenges without fear of judgment. By normalizing mistakes, we allow ourselves and others to grow more freely. When people know their errors won't lead to harsh criticism, they are more likely to take risks, try new things, and step outside their comfort zones. This openness promotes innovation and collaboration, which are essential for success in any endeavor.

The Journey of Continuous Improvement

Embracing imperfection is not about resigning ourselves to failure; instead, it's about committing to continuous improvement. Growth is a process that requires dedication and intentionality. The first step in personal development is having clear and well-defined goals. Vague goals can lead to confusion and lack of focus. When we know exactly what we want to achieve, staying on track is more accessible. Instead of saying, "I want to be better at praying," a more specific goal could be, "I will pray for 15 minutes every morning." This way, you know what you aim for and can measure your success. Ensure your goals align with your Christian values and what God calls you to do. For example, setting a goal to serve in a ministry or deepen your knowledge of the Bible can help you grow spiritually. A critical area of personal development is spiritual growth. As followers of Christ, growing in our faith is an ongoing journey.

Spiritual goals include reading the Bible regularly, praying daily, or becoming more active in church or ministry. One of the most important goals is to strengthen your relationship with God. In James 4:8, we are told, "*Draw near to God, and He will draw near to you.*" Setting goals that help you spend more time with God—such as prayer, Bible study, or worship—can deepen your faith. Another spiritual goal could be to serve others more, reflecting Christ's love. Matthew 20:28 says, "Just as the Son of Man did not come to be served, but to serve." Service is a crucial aspect of spiritual development, whether through acts of kindness, volunteering, or helping in your church.

Personal goals focus on your well-being, health, and character. Setting personal goals helps you become the best version of yourself, which benefits you and allows you to serve others more effectively. In Galatians 5:22-23, we learn about the fruit of the Spirit—love, joy, peace, patience, kindness, goodness, faithfulness, gentleness, and self-control.

Setting personal goals to grow in these areas can help you reflect Christ's character daily. Personal development also includes caring for your body, mind, and emotions. This could involve setting goals for regular exercise, a healthier diet, or time for rest, remembering that our bodies are temples of the Holy Spirit (1 Corinthians 6:19-20). Whether in school, working, or volunteering, setting professional or career-related goals is essential for growth. These goals help you improve your skills, advance your career, or take on new responsibilities. Colossians 3:23 encourages us to work *"with all your heart, as working for the Lord, not for human masters."*

Setting professional goals that help you give your best in your work or studies is a way to honor God. Sometimes, as we grow and change, our goals may need adjustment. This is a natural part of personal development. We must remain flexible, allowing God to guide us when new opportunities or challenges arise. Take time regularly to evaluate your progress and see if your goals align with what God is calling you to do. Changing your goals as you grow and God reveals new things to you is okay. Proverbs 16:9 says, "In their hearts, *humans plan their course, but the Lord establishes their steps."* While setting goals is essential, we must also trust that God may have a different or better plan for us.

Curiosity drives growth. When we're curious, we're eager to learn, explore new ideas, and ask questions. This thirst for knowledge keeps us open to discovering more about the world, ourselves, and God's plan for us. Be open to learning new things, whether it's through reading, taking a class, or having conversations with people who offer different perspectives.

Curiosity leads to creativity and innovation. Proverbs 18:15, *"The heart of the discerning acquires knowledge, for the ears of the wise seek it out."* We should never stop learning, as growth happens when we remain open to new experiences and ideas. Receiving feedback and incredibly constructive criticism can help us grow. While it might sometimes feel uncomfortable, feedback allows us to see areas we might have missed and helps us improve.

Embracing feedback is a vital part of developing a growth mindset. Instead of avoiding feedback, embrace it as an opportunity to grow. When someone points out an area of improvement, don't be discouraged—use it to refine your skills or actions. Proverbs 15:31, *"Whoever heeds life-giving correction will be at home among the wise."* Wisdom comes from being teachable and humble enough to listen to others' advice. Rather than seeing failure as a sign to stop, use it as a stepping stone.

Mistakes teach valuable lessons and help us move closer to success when we learn from them. Effort is essential in a growth mindset. It reminds us that success isn't only about talent, dedication, and hard work. We must be willing to put in the effort to grow, trusting that this effort will bear fruit over time. Ecclesiastes 9:10, *"Whatever your hand finds to do, do it with all your might."* Whether learning new skills, working on personal growth, or serving others, effort transforms potential into progress. Growth takes time. Sometimes, we won't see immediate results, but we can trust that we will improve over time with consistent effort and patience.

Fairness in Our Interactions
Embracing imperfection also extends to how we interact with others. Fairness is a fundamental principle that governs our relationships and communications. Fairness is at the heart of respectful and kind relationships. It involves treating others with dignity, acknowledging that we are all on unique growth paths, and recognizing that we each have our strengths and weaknesses.

Fairness requires us to show understanding, empathy, and equality in our interactions with others. Everyone's journey is different, and part of treating others with respect is acknowledging their paths. Some people may be more assertive in certain areas, while others may still be learning and growing.

Fairness encourages us to accept these differences without judgment and to offer support rather than criticism. We're all at different life stages; showing patience and understanding as others grow is essential. Proverbs 22:2, *"Rich and poor have this in common: The Lord is the Maker of them all."* God created us all equally, regardless of our backgrounds, talents, or challenges. Just as we appreciate others' strengths, we must be compassionate toward their weaknesses.

Treating people fairly means helping them where they need it, not holding their shortcomings against them. The Bible emphasizes that we should not show favoritism but treat everyone with equal love and respect. James 2:1: *"My brothers and sisters, believers in our glorious Lord Jesus Christ, must not show favoritism."* This means we should value everyone, regardless of status, appearance, or abilities. Whether someone is rich or poor, strong or weak, everyone deserves to be treated with kindness and respect. When we avoid favoritism, we create an atmosphere where all feel valued and appreciated. Colossians 3:11, *"Here there is no Gentile or Jew, circumcised or uncircumcised, barbarian, Scythian, slave or free, but Christ is all, and is in all."* In Christ, we are all equal, and we should reflect that equality in how we treat one another. Being fair, we help build relationships based on trust and mutual respect.

Fairness promotes harmony, cooperation, and support among people, allowing us to grow together. When we treat others with kindness and respect, we foster an environment where everyone feels safe and valued. Fair treatment builds trust, leading to more robust, cooperative relationships. In such an environment, people are more likely to help one another and work toward common goals.

As imperfect beings, we are bound to make mistakes and face challenges in our interactions with others. However, forgiving and understanding reflect God's grace and create an environment where healing and growth can flourish. We all fall short and make mistakes. It's important to remember that no one is perfect, and just as we make errors, so do others. This humility helps us approach situations with grace and understanding rather than harsh judgment.

Acknowledging that we are not perfect makes it easier to forgive others. We understand that, just as we desire forgiveness when we make mistakes, others deserve the same grace. Romans 3:23, *"For all have sinned and fall short of the glory of God."* Holding onto grudges can create bitterness in our hearts. Instead, practicing forgiveness frees us from resentment, allowing us to move forward in love and peace. Just as God extends grace to us, we are called to extend grace to others. When we show compassion and understanding to those who have wronged us, we demonstrate the love of Christ.

Forgiving someone is not always easy, but it's a decision that brings healing to both parties. Forgiveness also involves understanding that people may be struggling with their challenges. By being patient and compassionate, we can help them grow and heal. Christ's forgiveness was given without conditions or limits. In the same way, we are called to forgive others, even if they don't ask for it or repeat their mistakes. This kind of forgiveness releases us from the pain of holding onto past hurts. When we forgive, we open the door for healing. The person offering and receiving forgiveness is accessible from the chains of anger, bitterness, and regret. Forgiveness restores relationships and brings peace to our hearts.

CONCLUSION

Living A Victorious Life

Living a victorious life with God is not about chasing after fleeting moments of success or worldly recognition. It is about walking hand in hand with God every day, knowing that His presence, guidance, and power bring true victory. In God's eyes, victory is far more profound than achieving material goals or overcoming temporary challenges—it's about living with purpose, growing in faith, and reflecting His love and goodness in everything you do.

A victorious life is rooted in trust. Trusting God means believing His plans are far greater than anything you could plan for yourself. It means leaning on Him in times of uncertainty, relying on His wisdom when life's path is unclear, and being confident that He is working all things for your good. As you trust God more, you'll discover that victory comes not only through external achievements but through the inner peace, joy, and strength that only He can provide.

Victory is not a one-time event—it's a lifestyle. To live a victorious life, you must be consistent in your faith, always seeking God through prayer, reading His Word, and living out His principles. Consistency builds spiritual strength and keeps you grounded in the truth, no matter what comes your way. As you grow in spiritual maturity, you will find that the victories God gives you are not just for your benefit but are designed to help others. Maturity is about moving from being a receiver to being a giver—from learning to teaching, from being blessed to being a blessing.

A victorious life bears fruit not only in your own heart but in the lives of those around you. A fundamental principle of victory is generosity. When you live generously—sharing your time, resources, wisdom, and love—you open the door for God to do even more in your life. Generosity is a sign of spiritual victory because it reflects God's heart and allows you to impact the world in powerful ways.

Victory comes when you align your life with God's purpose. This means making decisions with integrity, living by God's principles, and pursuing His calling. Living purposefully means focusing on God's plan and not being easily swayed by distractions or setbacks. Integrity ensures that your victories are built on a solid foundation.

Life is filled with obstacles, but living a victorious life means overcoming those challenges with God's strength, not your own. It's about acknowledging that in your weakness, God's power is made perfect. When you rely on His strength, you can confidently face any situation, knowing that Christ already won the battle.

Living a victorious life starts with trusting God fully, walking in faith, and pursuing His purpose above all else. It's a commitment to follow where He leads, even when the road seems complex or unclear. But as you take that step of faith, you will discover that God will lead you to victory in every area of your life.

Victory in God's kingdom is not about perfection but progress. It's about continually pressing forward, learning from your mistakes, and trusting that God is shaping you into who He created you to be. There will be times of struggle, but remember that God's grace is sufficient. His power is at work in you, and as long as you stay connected to Him, you will continue to experience His victories. Ultimately, living a victorious life means understanding that Jesus Christ has already won your ultimate victory. His death and resurrection secured your eternal triumph over sin, death, and every obstacle in your way.

When you live in the light of this truth, every other victory becomes possible. With Christ as your source of strength, wisdom, and guidance, you can confidently walk through life, knowing that you are more than a conqueror. No matter what challenges you face, you can declare with certainty that you are victorious, not by your power, but by the power of God at work in you. So, as you move forward, embrace the victorious life that God has planned for you. Walk in faith, live with purpose, and trust in the One who can do abundantly more than you could ever ask or imagine. With God, victory is not just possible—it is inevitable.

A SPECIAL CALL TO SALVATION & NEW BEGINNINGS FROM APOSTLE DR. DAVID PHILEMON

Dear Beloved,

God loves you deeply and has brought you to this moment for a reason. No matter your past, His love and forgiveness are available to you.

The Bible says in John 3:16, "For God so loved the world that He gave His one and only Son, that whoever believes in Him shall not perish but have eternal life." Jesus Christ came to save you, offering you a new life of purpose and peace.

If you're ready to accept Jesus as your Lord and Savior, pray this simple prayer:

The Salvation Prayer

"Heavenly Father, I come to You in the Name of Jesus. I acknowledge that I am a sinner in need of a Savior. I believe that Jesus Christ is Your Son, that He died for my sins, and that You raised Him from the dead. I repent of my sins and turn to You with my

Whole heart. Jesus, I ask You to come into my life. Be my Lord and my Savior. I surrender my life to You. Fill me with Your Holy Spirit, guide me on the path of righteousness, and help me to follow Your script for my life. Thank you, Father, for saving me. In the name of Jesus. Amen."

Welcome to the Family of God!

If you have just prayed this prayer, Congratulations! You are now a child of God, and heaven is rejoicing. Your journey has begun, and we're here to support you as you grow in faith and discover God's unique plans for you.

Next Steps:
• Connect with a Bible-believing church.
• Read the Bible Daily: God's Word is your guide.
• Pray Regularly: Prayer is your lifeline to God.
• Share Your Faith: Don't keep the good news to yourself.

www.ingramcontent.com/pod-product-compliance
Lightning Source LLC
Chambersburg PA
CBHW071906020426
42331CB00010B/2701